Jacob's Journey
(From Playing T-Ball to Coaching Baseball)

Written by:
Dr. Dionne D. Nichols

Illustrations by Blueberry Illustrations

Copyright © 2022 by Dr. Dionne D. Nichols

All rights reserved.
No part of this book may be reproduced
or transmitted in any form or by any means
without written permission from the author.

979-8-218-03829-8

DEDICATION

This book is dedicated to my former high school classmate and friend Sharon Fink Poche. Thanks for allowing me to capture amazing stories of your son Jacob Snyder on his baseball journey.

Every summer Jacob watched his mom take his sister to softball practice and he could not wait to turn 5 years old so he could play T-Ball at the nearby park. However, the time finally came, and he began playing T-Ball to develop his ball-game skills and have fun. This did not come without challenges. Jacob was a scrawny kid who was not a good hitter due to his dominant left hand. On the other hand, this allowed him to catch and throw the ball better than all the other kids at the park.

His mom became his biggest cheerleader and at every game she would be the loudest in the bleachers yelling, **"Run Jacob, Run!"** after he would hit the ball.

Jacob's support system grew. His grandmother began practicing with him in the yard throwing the baseball as they would play pitch and catch.

Oftentimes, the yelling from Jacob's mom became so loud that he was embarrassed at hearing her say **"Run Jacob, Run"** during the T-Ball games.

Eventually, the "**Run Jacob, Run**" turned into **"Hit that ball Jacob"** as he progressed into the sport of baseball at high school. Jacob's work ethic increased. He developed a strong arm at throwing with his left hand and hitting the baseball with his right hand.

He practiced his pitching skills daily and Coach Kenny made sure he was the starting pitcher to end each game with all perfect innings. Jacob's improbable form and grit led him to win All District and a 5A-District Championship while playing high school baseball.

He practiced his pitching skills daily and Coach Kenny made sure he was the starting pitcher to end each game with all perfect innings. Jacob's improbable form and grit led him to win All District and a 5A-District Championship while playing high school baseball.

He practiced his pitching skills daily and Coach Kenny made sure he was the starting pitcher to end each game with all perfect innings. Jacob's improbable form and grit led him to win All District and a 5A-District Championship while playing high school baseball.

However, while every high school senior player on the school's baseball team began to prepare for graduation, Jacob aspired to go straight to the Major Baseball League (MLB). Unfortunately, this did not happen. One day, a college recruiter came to visit his best friend to play for a local college team. His best friend met with the recruiter but told him to check out Jacob's skills and form. The recruiter was so impressed that he offered Jacob a scholarship to play college baseball on the spot.

Within a few weeks, Jacob's family visited the beautiful college campus and baseball training facility. He fell in love! Jacob not only brought his unique skills to the college, but diversity as well. He played baseball amongst students that were a different race than him, but he was embraced for his love of baseball and his amazing skills.

Jacob's mom cheers became even louder for her son as she yelled, **"Throw that ball, Jacob!"** after every swing.

Jacob became a 2-time SWAC Champion during his time at college. He learned to embrace his mom's loud cheers as a sense of true support

Though right before he graduated college, they offered him a coaching position. Jacob graciously accepted the position. This position was an honor for him to serve.

Jacob's love for the sport allowed him to give back to other kids just like him and share his knowledge and journey of baseball.

Lesson Learned

"Hard work, grit, and determination pays off."

"Let your support system be the loudest cheers for you."

ABOUT THE AUTHOR

Dr. Dionne D. Nichols is an educator with over 20 years of experience in early childhood, elementary, secondary, and higher education. She holds a Bachelor of Arts degree in Elementary Education, a Master of Arts degree in Teaching in Urban Schools both from Southern University at New Orleans and a Master of Arts degree in Administration and Supervision from Nicholls State University, Thibodaux, LA. In addition, she has earned her doctorate degree in Educational Leadership and Administration from Capella University, Minneapolis, MN.

Dr. Nichols is presently a professor at Northwestern State University serving practitioners who are enrolled in Early Childhood Education and Teaching Grades 1-5 programs and she is an Independent Educational Consultant for Early Childhood and Special Education. She is a proud member of the Alpha Kappa Alpha Sorority, Inc.

Most recently, Dr. Nichols has written several children's books that depicts minority characters that all children can relate to. She is committed to the idea of life-long learning and believes that education is the key to success in life for both children and adults. More importantly, Dr. Nichols is dedicated to leading change in our schools and educational organizations.

DR. NICHOLS is active in both her church and community. She is the proud mother of her only daughter Shantrice and grandmother to her 5-year-old granddaughter Saige.

ABOUT THE AUTHOR

Dr. Dionne D. Nichols is an educator with over 20 years of experience in early childhood, elementary, secondary, and higher education. She holds a Bachelor of Arts degree in Elementary Education, a Master of Arts degree in Teaching in Urban Schools both from Southern University at New Orleans and a Master of Arts degree in Administration and Supervision from Nicholls State University, Thibodaux, LA. In addition, she has earned her doctorate degree in Educational Leadership and Administration from Capella University, Minneapolis, MN.

Dr. Nichols is presently a professor at Northwestern State University serving practitioners who are enrolled in Early Childhood Education and Teaching Grades 1-5 programs and she is an Independent Educational Consultant for Early Childhood and Special Education. She is a proud member of the Alpha Kappa Alpha Sorority, Inc.

Most recently, Dr. Nichols has written several children's books that depicts minority characters that all children can relate to. She is committed to the idea of life-long learning and believes that education is the key to success in life for both children and adults. More importantly, Dr. Nichols is dedicated to leading change in our schools and educational organizations.

DR. NICHOLS is active in both her church and community. She is the proud mother of her only daughter Shantrice and grandmother to her 5-year-old granddaughter Saige.

www.ingramcontent.com/pod-product-compliance
Lightning Source LLC
LaVergne TN
LVHW072116060526
838201LV00011B/253